BitCoins Revealed: How it works, Myths busted, Mining and strategies
Peter K. Black

Copyright © 2014 Pierre Jereczek

All rights reserved

To my readers and my wife

Table of Contents

Introduction to Bitcoins

Advantages of Bitcoin

How it works

Bitcoin Mining

The Future of Bitcoins

Myths

Conclusion

Introduction to Bitcoins

Bitcoins is the new gold rush of the present day. Many people are excited about a new currency that they can be able to use. The thrill of a currency that is completely digital fits perfectly into the average person's lifestyle, especially nowadays when we purchase and sell goods via digital money.

But learning how to earn bitcoins in order to spend is a bit more complex than explaining how to use a U.S. dollar bill. To the newcomer, the number of complex algorithms and mathematics that is incorporated into the bitcoin currency market is enough to say, "I give up".

Well that's where I come in with this eBook. We're going to take a full tour through the world of Bitcoins, step by step, in order for you to understand each concept clearly. You'll be able to leave this book with enough knowledge about this subject and hopefully help you gain a footstool in the market and make you start profiting and increase your bank account.

So before we dive into the intricate world of Bitcoins, let's look at an overview of what bitcoins are.

Fundamental of Bitcoins

First of all, there's a difference between 'Bitcoin' and 'bitcoins'. The word with a capitalized "B" refers to the whole market system itself. Similar to how the term 'Forex' refers to the market where different currency pairs are exchanged worldwide by professional traders. The word with a small letter "b" refers to the actual currency itself. Akin to the U.S. dollar, European Union euro and the Australian dollar are to the Forex market. As you can see, bitcoins aren't too far off to the currencies that people have been trading in the past to the present.

Now how bitcoins are incorporated into our society is by a network agreement worldwide that allows people to be able to purchase and sell with a currency that's entirely digitized. It is a completely decentralized payment network that is exchanged from peer to peer. This allows the bitcoin traders to use bitcoins without any central bank or middleman in between the currency exchanges. Now that we know that it's similar to our currencies that we regularly trade, let's pay respect to the person that made this currency.

Who created Bitcoin?

Bitcoin wasn't just created in one day. It started out as a paper that was submitted to an online publishing center in the year of 2008 by a man named Satoshi Nakamoto. The paper was titled "*Bitcoin: A Peer-to-Peer Electronic Cash System.* Satoshi's paper described how a currency exchanged on a peer-to-peer network could be used for electronic transactions without the need of a middleman. A year after the paper was published, Satoshi released his first version of the software client and many people were able to participate in the project.

As time passed by, the people that participated in the project began to increase and Mr. Satoshi Nakamoto himself began to fade away from his own creation. By the year of 2010, he completely disappeared from the picture. He was always careful not to reveal too many details about himself to other people.

There are certain claims that Mr. Satoshi Nakamoto is a 64 year old Japanese man, but the person that is "claimed" to be the creator has denied all allegations that he is the creator. Some people believe that the creator is actually a man named Michael Clear, a graduate cryptography student who studies at the Dublin's Trinity College. A *New Yorker's* Joshua Davis came to this conclusion after researching and analyzing over 80,000 words of Mr. Nakamoto's writings online.

There are also some other conclusions as to who the Bitcoin creator might actually be. But no one truly knows because the site bitcoin.org was registered on the date of August 18th, 2008, and the person that registered the website used an anonymous Japanese service and had it hosted with a Japanese ISP. So even though the site was registered through a service in Japan, that's not enough reason to assume that the creator would be Japanese, or even, called Satoshi Nakamoto.

All we know is that he had thought about this digital currency well and thoroughly before implementing it for experimentation in our society today. He wasn't a phenomenal code programmer, but that didn't stop his idea from continuing its progress. In any case, he had made a smart decision in using a pseudo name. That way, people could focus on the actual program rather than on the creator.

Now that we've taken a brief trip back in time, we can now come to the present and take a look at how bitcoin works and how it compares to the regularly traded currency.

Cryptography

We understand that Bitcoin is a virtual currency (digital) that has no tangible item that can be used to symbolize the actual currency rate i.e. coins, dollar bills, notes. It is the first and easiest currency that incorporates cryptography in its algorithms in order to control its creation, administration and security.

It's risen exponentially in value between the times that it was created to the present by more than $100 market value. So how much difference is there between bitcoin and the currencies traded in the forex market? How can you trade it? Where can you trade bitcoin?

There are many questions that you have but we're going to take it step by step. First let's take a look at the difference between bitcoin and forex currencies.

Conventional Currencies vs. Bitcoin

There are some fundamental ways that bitcoin compares to the conventional currencies traded on the forex market. Just for simplicity, we're going to use the U.S. dollar as a representation of all the currencies in the foreign exchange.

1. Bitcoins use a P2P (Peer-to-Peer) network that doesn't have a central authority

In other words, there is no centralization that is required when making a transaction. All the functions that a regular currency goes through such as issuance of the currency, processing of the transactions, and the verification process is completely removed in the bitcoin currency. All of these functions are carried out without any type of authority supervision. Everything is done within the P2P network.

In a U.S. dollar currency, the transactions are centralized by the central bank in order to control to control and maintain the national monetary policy. In the United States, the Federal Reserve has the power to issue money to the circulating market. They are the head honchos, the big daddy of the market. They supervise the banks, make sure that the financial system is stable, as well as provide financial services to the depository institutions. This kind of control is completely lacking in the bitcoin market.

2. Bitcoin is all digital

Although small companies are rising up with physical bitcoins, the currency is still primarily digitized. The physical coins that are made to represent the Bitcoins are similar to novelty items because they remove the purpose of having a digital currency. Comparing it to the U.S. dollar, dollar bills exist purposely because the currency is mostly in the physical form. If a person decided to convert all of his money from his bank account to dollar bills, he would be able to receive his money within a short time span if he so chooses.

3. There's a limit to the amount of bitcoins there are.

The total number of Bitcoins that will be issued to all the bitcoin traders is only 21 million. It seems like a lot but if we take a look at the calculation of how many bitcoins are created every 10 minutes, this amount of time that this cap number will be reached is very small. For every 10 minutes that passes, 25 bitcoins are created. Although the bitcoin currency is set to half the number of coins created in half every four years, it is estimated that by the year of 2140, the limit number will be reached.

This is a pretty risky fact to process because if the limit number is reached, then the bitcoin owners with the most percentage of the currency owned will have choices to make on whether to sell the currency or not. In terms of a currency's stability, this situation would be best avoided because if a said person had a large percentage of bitcoins owned and decided to exit the market by selling their share of bitcoins, the currency would experience heavy volatility. There would be multiple highs and lows within a short time span. Although currency traders prefer to have volatility in the market, the price spread would be too drastic and highly risky to any trader in the market.

This is where conventional currencies come in handy, because they don't have a limit to the amount of money that can be issued to anyone.

4.   Bitcoins are very complex.

The concept of cryptocurrency involves a lot of high level mathematics. This brings down the currency's usability towards the general population. In order to understand how and why Bitcoin works requires a high knowledge of mathematics and a high degree of technological knowledge. We're going to go over the cryptocurrency math in Bitcoins later on so that you can have a good grasp of the concept on how bitcoin truly works.

5.   Bitcoin isn't accepted in many places.

Since the currency is still relatively new, there aren't that many places that accept the currency. But the lists of companies that accept bitcoins are continuously increasing each month. The currency is spreading so fast that small businesses are trying to get some of the action. Even so, the only way that the bitcoin currency can be used when making a purchase is by scanning a QR code which requires a smart phone. Even though it seems that everyone has a smartphone, there are still some people that either don't use smart phones or simply don't have the time to learn how to use these kinds of functions on a smart phone. This is also a partial reason why the larger companies with management that has always stuck to the regular style of business prefer to stay that way because of the stability. They see this new currency as something that is still new and has many risks that come with it.

6. **There are some drawbacks to bitcoin transactions.**

The downfall to using bitcoins is that the transaction takes a bit long to process. The average amount of time that it takes for a transaction to be confirmed is about 10 minutes. This isn't fast by any means when compared to the time that it takes to use a conventional currency in a transaction. For example, when you pay for a meal at an Italian restaurant, the waiter will usually take the debit/credit card and the payment will be paid within seconds

Another drawback that bitcoin has is that the transactions are irreversible. The only way that it can be reversed is by getting a refund from the recipient of the bitcoin themselves. Currencies such as the U.S. dollar can be reversed if there is a valid reason by the money lender. There's no need to rely on the recipient's generosity.

7. **There's no insurance to your money**

When you make an account with a bank, they will usually insure your money of up to $250,000 and above in case there is a crisis where money is lost from the banks control. This is a relief cushion that is guaranteed with conventional money. When using bitcoins on the other hand, there's no protection. If someone was to steal your hard drive, hack into your computer and steal all of your bitcoins from your digital wallet, there you would be no way of retrieving it back.

Advantages of Bitcoin

The previous points that we've made highlight only a few of the differences between the conventional currency vs the Bitcoin. But let's take a look at how the bitcoin is advantageous:

- **No Third-Party Interferences**

No redundancies in the market transaction log database. No one is able to take any bitcoins simply by hacking into the database and taking it all for themselves. The only way that a third party can force a bitcoin user to give them their money is by other means, such as sending the money to someone else.

- **No Taxes**

One of the best features that attract many traders and investors to the Bitcoin market is that there are no taxes that are imposed on the bitcoins. The only way that a bitcoin owner can face any taxes is if the person sends a percentage of the bitcoin amount that is sent in the transaction specifically for tax purposes.

- **No Tracking**

There's no way that someone can be able to track a specific person from a transaction that they made from their wallet addresses. Even though there's a log that shows a transaction took place, only the transaction is shown, but not the specific details and personal information about a bitcoin trader. Also no one knows how many bitcoins are in a trader's wallet except the owner himself. Even if the wallet's address was publicly shared, a new address can be created easily. This is a method that can increase the privacy of a trader when comparing to conventional currency systems.

- **No Extra Fees on Transactions**

Receiving and sending bitcoins doesn't require any extra cost towards the bitcoin owner because in order to perform these transactions, the Bitcoin client is required to keep running and stay connected to the other nodes. Basically, when bitcoin users use their bitcoins, they are in return helping the network remain functional and share the burden of authorizing the other transactions. This type of sharing has reduced the transaction costs significantly to the point where they are completely irrelevant.

- **Lack of "chargeback" Risks**

The moment bitcoins are sent away from an owner's wallet, the transaction cannot be reversed. The reason is because the bitcoins that are sent will be the recipient's bitcoins. They will claim ownership of the coins. There's no way of returning money that is officially another party's bitcoin. The recipient's party has the private key and only they are able to decide whether they want to give a return or not.

- **Stealing is a bit difficult**

The only ways that someone's bitcoins can be stolen is by stealing the physical access to a bitcoin owner's computer, and use it to send bitcoins to their own accounts. There is a possibility of a person stealing your phone, or hacking into one of your wallets. But the chances of that happening are pretty slim because they would have to go through a large amount of computations that need to be solved in order to steal the account. So there is a chance that a hacker can be able to steal your bitcoins, but the chances of that happening are very low. The conventional currencies are a lot easier for access to bank accounts due to the low amount of authentication processes that need to be bypass to gain access to an account holder's finances.

We've seen that there are a lot of benefits to using the conventional currency versus the newer bitcoins. But nevertheless, the currency is still in its infant years. Possibly in the next 20 years or so, there will be more security and encryption that will protect your bitcoins from any hackers. Also at that time, there will be more companies that will accept the use of the currency in their business transactions.

How it works

Before we get into the more technical mathematics of how bitcoin works, let's get an overview of how it works.

Let's begin understanding bitcoins from a standpoint where you haven't put your feet into the waters to get a personal feel of the market. The first step that you'd have to do is to sign up and set a new digital wallet on your computer or your mobile device. Getting a wallet is completely free since it's from a free, open source software program that will generate your first and future Bitcoin addresses. You'll be using this to store your bitcoins.

When you make a wallet, there are three types: A software wallet that is installed on your computer, a mobile wallet that is installed on your mobile device, and a web wallet which is located on the website that hosts the bitcoins that people have earned.

Now the way that the bitcoin security is setup is by a public key encryption4 technique. What this means for the bitcoin trader is that when they get a new Bitcoin address created, they will have a cryptographic key pair that has two different keys: a public and a private key. These keys are long, unique strings of letters and numbers that are generated with the creation of the address.

Each address that is created has its own Bitcoin balance. This way the trader only has to worry about is acquiring the number of bitcoins that are held at one of these addresses in your designated wallet. There are many ways that you can gain bitcoins: they can be purchased from a Bitcoin currency exchange i.e. Mt. Gox, Bitstamp. They can also be received from a service such as BitInstant where the funds are able to be transferred between Bitcoin exchanges. This service also supports different methods of payments.

Now the one thing to note about Bitcoin transactions is that they are all public and are permanently recorded on the Bitcoin network. This means that there is no privacy with any purchases or sales that are made by anyone who owns bitcoins. Each balance and transactions that are made are completely visible to everyone. It might be a bit embarrassing when everyone can be able to see what you've purchased. In order to counter this, the professionals recommend that everyone who owns bitcoins should create a new address for each transaction that they make. This will ensure privacy and also bring more security towards the trader.

After making your own bitcoin address and acquiring your own bitcoins, you can now use them to go online and make purchases on goods that you'd like to have from companies that accept Bitcoins as an optional payment method. The way this works is that the company will send you the Bitcoin address where you will send your Bitcoin payment. Do you see how the Bitcoin address is used? When you send the payment to the address, the transaction will usually take about a few seconds to happen, but the verification process will take about 10 minutes or even longer.

Bitcoins is simply an optional method of gaining money that can be used for commercial use. A small thing to remember is that Bitcoin transactions, with no exceptions whatsoever, are included in a log that is records all the transactions and is openly shared to the public. This log is called a "block chain". This recording method is to clarify that the party that spent the Bitcoins truly owns them, and aren't using any fraudulent type of bitcoins.

So the question arises is, why does the verification process take so long. The answer is because bitcoins involve many complex algorithms that are in Bitcoin mining. Solving these complex algorithms takes time, and needs a lot of computing power at one's disposal.

Let's take a look at why it takes so long to solve these math problems that are incorporated into the bitcoin currency.

Bitcoin Mining

The bitcoin network consists of thousands of machines that all run the Bitcoin software. The network itself has two main tasks that it needs to do: Relay the information from the transaction that a bitcoin owner has made and verify those transactions on their legitimacy. The second task is to make sure that the bitcoin is not spent more than once. This way the number of bitcoins in circulation are all accounted for.

The first task that needs be done is accomplished very easily by the Bitcoin network via the P2P network. There are many nodes that are spread all over the globe. These nodes are operated in order to for the network to make sure that it will always function as long as it brings a useful service.

The second task that needs to be done is the more complex and mathematical section of the bitcoin equation. The process that occurs in this area is called mining, similar to how coal miners used to mine for coal back in the Industrial evolution. This process is carried out by multiple computers that have large computing power to run the mining software.

Let's take a look at the specific reasons as to why bitcoin traders need to mine for bitcoins. We'll also take look at the different techniques used to mine bitcoins and also look at other ways of safely storing and using the digital currency.

Reason for mining

There are many reasons why people mine for bitcoins. Some people mine because the already have the knowledge that it takes in order to compute the complex mathematical equations needed to obtain bitcoins. These bitcoin traders often work or have a background in a field that overlaps with the way that bitcoins work. For example, if a person works with grid computations, then they'd be able to enjoy bitcoin mining because grid computing are fun to do and require people to work together in order to solve a larger problem.

People who are in the technology fields have been used to being innovative in their work and see new opportunities when looking at the bitcoin currency. They usually like to keep up with the ever-changing technology world. Bitcoin for example is a large project that involves different types of technologies such as: cryptography, peer-to-peer networks and largely distributed databases. Some bitcoin users prefer to learn something new and build personal experience by attempting mining.

Another reason why some people mine for bitcoins is because they gain a profit from mining. It's not an easy business because just like the forex market, the prices of Bitcoins can fluctuate with high volatility in a short time span. There are also other investment costs that can accumulate to the thousands. The best way to make a profit from this market would be to find a way to efficiently mine for enough profits that can cover the expenses first before any large purchases are made.

Why Bitcoin Prices Fluctuate So Much

The many price fluctuations that occur in the Bitcoin market are drive by a lot of factors. One of the factors that drive most of these effects is the high amount of volatility. The volatility is Bitcoin doesn't really have a general index that is acceptable by many of the traders since it is a cryptocurrency and is still in its infant stages as an asset class. An example of how volatile the bitcoin market moves is by looking at 2013's price movements. Within one year, the price jumped from $100 to $1,240 with the peak at the end of December 2013. The amount of price changes that happens in the bitcoin market is 10 times as much as the price fluctuates in the conventional market i.e. U.S. dollar. There are other factors that all play a part in driving the price of the Bitcoin currency. Examples of these are:

The adoption rate of the currency is weakened by adverse press news:

Adverse news that brings fear to the bitcoin users includes the political news from different nations and also statements by governments that are claiming to bring regulation towards the bitcoin market. News that brought fear to the bitcoin traders was the bankruptcy of Mt. Gox in the early 2014 as well as the drug transactions that were found through Silk Road which ended when the FBI intervened and shutdown the whole marketplace in the month of October 2013. Both those incidents caused large fluctuation in the price of the market. However, the bitcoin investors saw a ray of hope by looking at the bad news as a way that the bitcoin market is maturing, bringing the value of the bitcoins against the dollar back up in price within a short period.

Bitcoin's apparent value alters:

One of the reasons why bitcoin swings against the conventional currencies is because of the apparent value that bitcoin has against the conventional currency. There are a lot of properties that Bitcoin has that are close or even similar to gold. The currency is governed by the developers of the core technology in order to limit its production to a fixed amount, which is 21 million BTC. Since this number is completely differs from the conventional currency which is managed by governments who want to maintain a low inflation, high employment rates and a satisfactory growth process, if the national economies built with the forex currencies show signs of weakness, investors change how much of their money they have placed in the conventional currencies and into the Bitcoin market.

Changes in the intrinsic value of the Bitcoin market

Bitcoin's volatility also stems from the many perceptions towards its intrinsic value of the cryptocurrency as a store of value and a method of value transfer. The store of value is defined as the function in which an underlying asset can be of use in the future by prediction. A store of value is able to be saved and exchanged for either goods or service sometime in the future. A method of value transfer is defined as any object that is used to send property in the form of assets from one person to another. With the large volatility that Bitcoin has in its markets, it's very hard to accurately describe what the store of value is, but it reveals a near frictionless value transfer. When these two parts of the intrinsic value differ, the bitcoin's value can fluctuate very rapidly when there's a news event.

Very little option value to large holders of the currency:

The volatility of the bitcoin market is also driven by the holders that have large amounts of bitcoins that are part of the total outstanding float of the currency. For the bitcoin investors, the current total amount of holdings is around $10M. There's no possible way of traders with that large amount of money to remove it from the market and liquidate it into a conventional currency without causing a severe movement in the bitcoin price movement. Since bitcoin's volume is but a small representation of the small cap, the currency hasn't reached its maximum levels that would be needed to provide some optional choices for the large holders of the bitcoin currency.

Security breaches

The bitcoin market gets very volatile when the bitcoin community exposes different vulnerabilities as a way for them to make massive open source responses in the form of security fixes. This is a very paradox way for the security to produce large outcomes, with so many difference open source software that take most of the credit such as Linux. When the bitcoin developers see concern between the bitcoin traders, they have to reveal solutions to them in order to alleviate the fear that they have from the security concerns.

There was a recent OpenSSL vulnerability attack by a bug called the Heartbleed that was reported by a Google security team member, Neel Mehta in April 1, 2014 brought a bearish market towards the bitcoin market price. The market dropped more than 10% for the month of April in that year against the U.S dollar. The fact that bitcoin and open source software development are both built on the same foundation that is free for the public to be able to examine and change to their preference. With this said, the bitcoin community is held responsible for any issues that may arise with the design of the software. Whenever the community resolves an issue with the bitcoin software, the bitcoin market responds with a higher level of confidence.

The investment of bitcoins and direct foreign investments in countries with high inflation

Bitcoins use the currency from the developing countries that have high inflation is very valuable in the volatility of the bitcoin markets when comparing it to the volatility of the bitcoin in U.S. dollars. There's a lot more versatility when the bitcoin is against the US dollar that the peso against the U.S. dollar that has a high inflation.

The Future of Bitcoins

The bitcoin currency has many promising qualities that can be beneficial for the economy. But at the same time, there are many drawbacks that just don't cut it in todays' fast paced world. The fact that the verification process takes longer than the regular conventional currency is something that might need to get changed or altered in order for it to continue being the success that it has been for the past five years.

In order to see what the future of Bitcoins will be, let's take a trip down memory lane. Remember when you made your first AOL account when dial-up speeds were the top of the line speeds? What about your first email? There are many things that we experienced back in the 2000s that were the stepping stones to what we have today. Most of those things were considered to be futuristic items that would take a while for the larger population to catch on. Well, they caught on real quick didn't they? What do you think of bitcoins?

They could be the next "internet" phenomenon. Just like when the internet was introduced when dial-up connection was the fastest speed available. At that time it was a revolutionary thing that was amazing but way ahead of its time. Look at how we work today. People are able to stream videos, order food, turn off their cars from miles away, talk to their parents on skype and check their email, all while sitting on their couches at 2pm in the afternoon. The world was completely changed.

Bitcoin is another ahead-of-its-time product.

It may look very disastrous at this moment but soon enough people will catch on and the next thing you know people will be running their companies and exchanging large amounts of currency with a swipe of their fingers over their phones or something like that.

Even so bitcoin can completely fail and end up like the startup companies that didn't get a chance to last for a long period of time. But if it succeeds, then the world will be completely revolutionized. The amazing invention that was brought with Bitcoin isn't the currency itself but rather the publicly distributed block chain, or ledger. The block chain is a public data structure that is shared by all the nodes (miners) that participate in the trading bitcoin network. The block chain includes every single transaction that was ever made with the cryptocurrency, making all of the coins traceable.

The bitcoin ledger can be used for much more areas. It can be used as a voting system, file storage, SSL verification authorities and even API. Once the public catches on the versatility that the block chain has to offer, people will be open to the idea of taking the technology of Bitcoin and using it on various ideas and projects. The wonderful part of the block chain is that it is pseudo-anonymous and simultaneously traceable.

So how will this be implemented into our society? Here are some examples of how the block chain will help people with in their daily lives:

Payday

My payment from my job is direct deposit, and it's scheduled to take 2 business days before it's actually "in" my bank account. With the block chain implemented, payment can be made within the same day. No need of waiting for the money in order to pay the bills. You can be able to have your money at a faster speed than before.

Government

The block chain can be used in developing countries that have a large population that are poor. Governments in these countries can be able to use the block chain when collecting their taxes. The can also use the public ledger in order to audit all the citizens for a low cost and also reduce the corruption that tends to always linger within governments of each country.

Voting

During the Election Day, there's always a news report stating that there was a voting fraud. How would the public ledger help in this area? Every person that is eligible to vote would be assigned an address. The votes would be short, quick and accurate. There won't be any issues of voting frauds or mistakes. This might even increase the number of voters.

Business to Business

This is the perfect place for the bitcoin public ledger to be used. There wouldn't be any fees in the transactions between individuals and businesses together from the local areas to overseas. Companies such as Amazon and eBay send large sized transactions with multiple companies all across the globe. Just how much money would they save if they utilized the block chain?

So there are plenty of opportunities that bitcoin will open up for other transactions in our society and change the way businesses will function entirely. There's much potential with Bitcoin, but the part with the most potential is the public ledge that has been introduced by bitcoin.

Myths

There's a long list of myths that revolve around what bitcoins are. We're going to cover twenty-eight of these myths here and debunk each one.

Myth #1: Bitcoin is just another conventional currency

Truth: Bitcoin is a cryptocurrency with no central authority controlling it. All of the currencies that are controlled centrally can be printed by the controllers and can be destroyed with an attack towards the central authorities.

There are no rules that are imposed toward the bitcoin currency, unlike the other currencies i.e. U.S. dollar, European Union euro. Without any centralization, Bitcoin is able to function without any of these issues.

Myth #2: Bitcoins don't help solve any problems that conventional currency can't solve

Truth: Bitcoin is a very versatile currency because it can be transferred from person to person without any transaction fees, it is very secure in terms of theft protection, verification process takes a few minutes but nonetheless is very efficient, and it can be granulated easily.

Also, there's a predictable number of supply to the bitcoin currency. It's not controlled by a Federal Reserve or any central banks and it isn't debt based. Bitcoins really have a lot of benefits and solve more problems that regular currencies have. As an addition to the previous benefits, bitcoin is an anonymous currency that protects the identity of an owner, there's no chance of the currency being frozen, easy to transfer and is cheap to make the transfer transactions.

Myth #3: Just like how the U.S. dollar was backed by gold, Bitcoin is backed by processing power.

Truth: It is incorrect to say that the bitcoin currency is backed by a computer processing power. When a currency is backed by something, it means that it I pegged, attached, to something else that is in control from an authority at a specific exchange rate. Bitcoins can't be exchanged for computing power. It doesn't make any sense for that to happen. So bitcoin isn't backed by anything. It is simply a currency by itself.

The bitcoin currency is *created* by a processing power and the block chain characteristic that it has is *protected* by the large peer-to-peer network of all the bitcoin traders as well as the computing nodes from certain type of attacks.

Myth #4: Bitcoins are worthless. With no backing, it's simply nothing.

Truth: Many people could also bring the argument that gold isn't backed by anything either. Bitcoins have certain properties that allow it to subjectively valued by each individual. The valuation is demonstrated when a person is allowed to freely exchange and receive bitcoins.

Myth #5: How the Bitcoin value is calculated is by basing it off of the amount of electricity and computing power that it takes to mines it.

Truth: This statement was made in order to address the labor theory of value towards the Bitcoin. This rule is commonly accepted as a false statement. Just because an item, say item Z takes a certain amount of resources to make it doesn't mean that the product will be the same worth as the resources value.

As a matter of fact, bitcoins is the complete opposite of what the labor theory states. The cost to mine the bitcoins is based on the worth of the currency itself. If the bitcoins value increases, more people will mine and it'll be more difficult to mine because the cost of mining will increase as well. Likewise when the value of bitcoin decreases, the easier it is to mine the currency. This effect balances out because the cost of mining is inversely proportional to the value of bitcoins that are made.

Myth #6: No intrinsic value.

Truth: This isn't true. Each bitcoin that an individual bitcoin trader holds has the capability of taking a large number of short transaction messages in an international global business distribution and time stamped to a permanent data store.

Although there is a drawback between the amount of messages and how quickly they are embedded, it's still fair to say that one bitcoin allows a total amount of 1000 such messages to be embedded. Each one takes about 10 minutes to send since the fee is an insignificant amount totaling 0.001 BTC. This is enough to cover the fees to send the messages and get them confirmed quickly. This type of message sending has an intrinsic value because it shows the ownership of a specific document at a certain time period. This is proven by a one-way hash of the document within the transaction. When you consider the fees that are charged to use the electronic notarization service, close to $10 per document, then the intrinsic value of bitcoins would be close to $10,000 per bitcoin. That's a large amount of value for a currency that just started not too long ago.

There are other tangible commodities that have an intrinsic value which are usually less than its actual trading price. An example would be gold. If it wasn't using the inflation-proof type of value, then it wouldn't have the type of value of where it stands today because the industrial requirements for gold are a lot smaller than the amount of gold that is available in supply.

Even though throughout history the intrinsic value has generally helped to establish certain commodities as mediums of exchange, together with other characteristics i.e. scarcity, fungibility, durability and divisibility, it isn't necessary to have it. This is the reason that is used when in the statements that accuse bitcoins for not having any intrinsic value. The way that bitcoins make up for this lack of qualities is by using the possession of other qualities that are necessary for it to be a good medium of exchange, either equal in value or better than the actual commodity money.

Another way that this can be explained is by considering the value of bitcoin within the global network, instead of each bitcoin in isolation. The value of a single bitcoin derives from the global network of the bitcoin merchants, wallets, exchanges and anything else that uses bitcoins. A bitcoin is necessary for transmission of the economic information through the network.

The intrinsic value of anything is ultimately decided by looking at what the consumers are willing to trade an item for – supply and demand.

Myth #7: Bitcoin is illegal because there isn't any legal tender

Truth: Bitcoins are not illegal because there are a number of currencies that have existed prior to the creation of bitcoin that have no official government backings. In the year of 2013, the United States Financial Crimes Enforcement Network (FCEN) issued a brand new set of guidelines that were focused on currencies that are virtual and are decentralized. This enactment was more than likely targeting the bitcoin currency. Under these new set of rules, it states that a user of a virtual currency is not a Money Services Businesses (MSB) under the Financial Crimes Enforcement Network guidelines. Because of this fact, they don't have to go under any MSB registration, reporting or even keeping record of the regulations. Bitcoin miners, when they mine for their bitcoins for their own gain, they don't have to register with the MSB or the Money Transmitter.

A currency is just nothing but a convenient way to represent a unit of an account. Even if the national laws differ in many countries, bitcoin traders always check the laws of their jurisdiction in order to avoid anything that isn't under the law. Usually, trading commodities, digital currencies such as Bitcoins, game currencies like the World or Warcraft in-game currency are completely legal. This proves that Bitcoin is completely legal and okay to use.

Myth #8: Bitcoin is a type of domestic terrorism because it can harm the economic stability of a country and its currency

Truth: This isn't the case with bitcoins. In accordance to the actual definition of terrorism, in order for an act to be deemed as a terrorist attack, the party would need to perform violent activities that would be considered terrorist motives for legal purposes. Any recent remarks that have been made by politicians have no foundation in the law or fact.

Bitcoin is completely domestic and is not by any means a domestic terrorist attack in any country that uses this currency. Bitcoin is an international community that strives for the better of society. Regular businesses are adopting this currency and allowing customers to use them to make purchases.

Myth #9: Those that join the bitcoin market are trying to avoid taxes and this in turn will bring the downfall of a country's economy.

Truth: Some people claim that the tax evading traders that are joining the Bitcoin market will eventually lead to the downfall of civilization. This is but an extreme look at the probabilistic situation. It would take a lot more than a few tax evaders to take down all of civilization that was built through decades of progress.

The cash transactions that are made in regular commerce are usually held at the same level of concealment but are still taxed successfully. It's up to the individual to follow the state laws that are applicable in the home country or else they may face certain consequences.

Dealing with bitcoins, the transfer process of the currency can also be done anonymously, but spending them on any other kind of money anonymously is just as difficult as spending them on tangible items that are anonymous. People that avoid taxes are usually the ones that have inconsistencies in the way they live and the amount of income that they report.

Myth #10: Bitcoins can be printed by anyone. Therefore the currency is worthless.

Truth: The bitcoin currency is completely digitized. It can't be printed or minted like the conventional currencies can. The way the currency works is that bitcoin miners look for blocks that are in turn exchanged for a profit on the miner's efforts. A specific amount of bitcoins are awarded for the number of blocks that are mined. The transaction fees are paid by the other miners.

Therefore the bitcoin isn't actually worthless. It just can't be printed by just anyone because there is no tangible representative unit that can be used for commerce in the bitcoin currency.

Myth #11: The cryptography that Bitcoin is based on isn't proven, deeming the bitcoin a suspicious currency.

Truth: There are two certain algorithms that are used in the Bitcoin currency, SHA256 and ECDSA, are endorsed and standardized. SHA256 is actually used by the US government and is standardized by under the FIPS180-3 Secure Hash Standard. If a person doesn't trust these algorithms, then they wouldn't trust any credit card transactions or any other type of electronic banking transactions because they all include these algorithms in their systems. The bitcoin currency has a sound cryptography that is commonly accepted and understood by multiple parties all across the globe.

Myth #12: The early bitcoin traders are rewarded unfairly.

Truth: The notion that traders who started at the beginning of the Bitcoin rush are unfairly awarded is false. In fact, the early adopters of the currency are well awarded for risking their time and money into a brand new currency. The capital that was invested in bitcoin during its pre-natal stages helped to expand the community and take the currency through multiple milestones. The early bitcoin traders are part of the reason why the currency still exists today. Saying that they don't get rewarded properly is similar to saying that the stock investors who purchased stocks during a company's initial public offering are unfairly rewarded.

Also looking at the amount of publicity that bitcoin got in 2013, there's no reason why anyone who didn't invest in bitcoin at that time can complain. Anyone who would like to invest in the bitcoins at this moment would also be considered as an early bitcoin trader because within the next few years to come, they'll be able to see their investments profit when the price of the currency increases in value (potentially).

Myth #13: There needs to be more coins than just 21 million in order for a currency to continue functioning for a long time.

Truth: Breaking down the number of atomic units in a bit coin goes like this:

1 Bitcoin is divisible to eight decimal places. There are over two quadrillion possible atomic units in the bitcoin system. The value of 1 Bitcoin is a representation of 100,000,000 of these atomic units. So each bitcoin is divisible by up to 10^8.

When you look at the value of the unit of 1 Bitcoin and how its value grew to the extent that it wasn't useful in the day to day transactions, traders began to deal with smaller units such as milli-bitcoins or micro-bitcoins.

So there will always be coins that people can be able to mine before the 21 million limit is reached. There's no need for more bitcoins than the way it is at this moment.

Myth #14: Since bitcoins are stored inside a wallet file, can't you just copy and paste the files in order to get more coins?

Truth: It isn't possible to simply copy and paste bitcoins because the wallet has discrete keys that give you the rights to spend the bitcoins. It's the same as thinking of how a bank has your details stored in a file. If you give your bank information to another person, it won't double the amount of information in your account. You can share your money with others or they can go and spend your money; there's no chance of both situations happening at the same time.

Myth #15: The fact that you can lose your bitcoins and can't retrieve it in any way is a bad flaw in the bitcoin currency.

Truth: A fact about bitcoins is that they are divisible to 1×10^{-8}, so if your coins were lost, it wouldn't be the worst thing possible because the loss of your coins would in turn raise the value of all the other coins in circulation. A fewer bitcoins remaining in the currency market is not a big problem for the currency itself.

So why isn't there a method that can help to replace lost coins in the Bitcoin system? The answer to that is that it is close to impossible to differentiate a lost coin and one that is in a person's wallet unused.

Myth #16: The bitcoin market is another Ponzi scheme.

Truth: A Ponzi scheme is defined as when the founders of a company sway the investors to invest more of their money in order for them to profit. Bitcoin on the other hand doesn't have this kind of setup. With Bitcoins there is no central authority that is using the investors to profit for themselves. It's only about individuals who are trying to build an economy.

With a Ponzi scheme, the early adopters are the ones that usually make most of the profit from the investors that come in later on. In those schemes, the late investors are always on the losing side. Bitcoin on the other hand can have a win-win situation. For example, the early adopters can make a profit from the rise in price value. As the price value increases and more traders have a better understanding of how bitcoin works, they will later take the profits from the brand new and reliable currency with advantages that trump the current conventional currencies.

Side note, the creator of bitcoin, never spent any bitcoins at the early stages of this currency. The proof is in the block chain of the currency. This shows that he wasn't making this currency to be set up as a Ponzi scheme.

Myth #17: The deflation potential for Bitcoin is very high since there's a finite amount of coins. With coins being lost also doesn't help in the problem.

Truth: Even though there is a deflation force that is potentially possible of occurring, human factors help to offset the economic factors such as hoarding. This factor is able to reduce the chances of a deflation dilemma.

Myth #18: No control of inflation equates to a faulty currency.

Truth: Inflation is defined as a rise of prices over time, which results from the devaluation of a currency. The balance between supply and demand plays a part in the inflation of prices. If the supply of bitcoins stays fixed at a certain amount, then the only chance of inflation occurring is if the demand for bitcoins completely disappears. The total number of bitcoins that are available is capped at 21 million which isn't that much when compared to the other conventional currencies. This could bring a temporary inflation towards the rapid adoption of the Fractional Reserve Banking. But it will be stabilized once a substantial amount of bitcoins is stored in the reserves of banks.

Bitcoin is established to be a currency that is in the form of a distributed system. This means that if the demand of bitcoins was to deplete to near zero levels, then the currency would be doomed without any hope. The main point here is that bitcoin is a currency that can't be inflated by a single individual or party, like the government, because there isn't any way that the supply can be increased past its limits. The most likely scenario is that if Bitcoin becomes too popular that the demand rises to a level that is too much for the market, then the currency would increase in value until the demand stabilizes.

Myth #19: The bitcoin community consists of people that are anarchist and conspiracy theorists.

Truth: This is far from the truth because the members of the bitcoin community, despite their differences in their ideologies, still stand as one unit that strive to better the economic effect of the virtual currency. Bitcoin is comprised of a large number of regular people who either would like to reduce the costs of currency transactions or reduce the friction within the international e-commerce.

Myth #20: Anyone with the right amount of computing power can take over the network.

Truth: As time progresses there market will become harder and harder to be able to take over the network. At the moment the bitcoin network's computing power is way ahead of its time. In fact they are a lot better than most of the fastest supercomputers combined.

Even if a hacker was able to take over the network, they wouldn't be able to do much because they can't create fraud bitcoins, or take anyone else's money. An attacker's capabilities are very limited when the costs of performing all the functions of the bitcoin market will make them lose money in the long run rather than gaining profits.

Myth #21: Bitcoin is violating the rules that national governments have set.

Truth: There is no regulation in the bitcoin market.

Myth #22: After the cap limit is reached, no one will be able to generate any more bitcoin blocks

Truth: At the time that it'll take for the operating costs not to be covered by the bock chain creation bounty, then miners will be able to earn some profit from transaction fees. But otherwise, when the cap limit is reached, there will be other methods of payment that people will be able to use instead of generating bitcoin blocks.

Myth #23: With bitcoins, there's no way of getting a refund from a purchase. If there aren't any refunds available, this currency won't work in our society.

Truth: Have chargebacks on purchases is a method that is used to limit fraudulent activities. The person who is handling the purchase money is responsible for preventing any fraud. For example, if you bought something on eBay and the seller never shipped it, then PayPal would take the funds from the seller's account in order to return the money back to the buyer. This feature strengthens the eBay economy because the customers are able to see that their risk in purchasing items and not receiving their goods is lowered significantly and is safe.

With Bitcoin having no chargebacks, this helps the buyer to have more control over their money. The money that you own is yours and yours alone. No one is able to take it away from you without your consent.

Myth #24: Quantum computers would be able to break the Bitcoin's security.

Truth: While this may be true, quantum computers don't exist yet and probably won't exist for a long time. Bitcoin's security, when it's used in the proper way, depends on a lot more than just a few encryption keys. They are a lot harder to break. The security was designed to be upgraded if there was a potential threat that was imminent.

Myth #25: It's a waste of energy and harmful to the natural ecosystem.

Truth: Bitcoin mining is a very competitive and dynamic market. When setting up a mining rig, the process is very simple and can be dismantled with ease. The market is always pushing the bitcoin mining activity towards where the marginal price of electricity is either low or zero.

The electrical products used for bitcoin mining are very cheap for a reason. Electricity is difficult to transport, store and there is a low demand and high supply. Using electricity in this way I saw a lot less wasteful than just plugging in a mining rig.

The market forces could possibly push mining into innovative solutions that will be able to be efficient in using electricity with consumption level s close to zero. Mining bitcoins produces more heat per energy used. This is why bitcoin mining takes a bit longer to gain the bitcoins.

Myth #26: Store owners can't set any prices because of the volatility of the bitcoin currency.

Truth: The assumption is that bitcoins have to be sold immediately in order for the store owners to cover their expenses. But that is not the truth. If store owners used bitcoins as a payment method for their currencies, then they would be able to avoid the transaction fees and save more money. As time progresses, the volatility in the forex market is bound to decrease as the size of the market expands and grows.

Meanwhile, merchants would simply have to constantly pull the latest exchange rate in order to update their store prices.

Myth #27: Bitcoin is the perfect money system for criminals to use, which will lead to the currency being shut down.

Truth: Payment methods such as PayPal, Visa, and MasterCard are all ways that criminals can utilize in their businesses and avoid getting caught for a long period of time. The reason why this is the case is because our society runs on these cash payment methods and shutting them down would be cause the downfall of the economies themselves.

Bitcoin is continuously growing in size and will soon reach the point where no single organization will be able to ruin the network by any criminal activity.

Myth #28: Bitcoin will be shut down soon. Just like Liberty Dollars was.

Truth: Liberty Dollars was a commercial project that was created to set an alternative to the U.S. currency, not just digitally but also with the physical units i.e. coins, banknotes and dollars that are backed by precious metals. Of course there's nothing illegal with this approach that would cause it to be shut down. The only reason why Liberty Dollars was shut down was because violated some counterfeiting laws when their silver coins resembled the US currency.

Bitcoins is not in any way similar to that because it has no physical representation of the currency. It is completely digitized as well, which is completely different than what Liberty Dollars had. If Bitcoin was to be shutdown, it won't be an easy process because it is decentralized and there's no office, servers, office or anything tangible that can be removed by force.

Conclusion

Hopefully you've got a good understanding of how bitcoin works. We've seen the history of how Bitcoin originated and the purpose of its creation. Bitcoin has changed the way that purchases are made in the e-commerce trade. Bitcoin currency has taken the fees that are included in transactions away and brought a ledger that keeps track of each transaction that is made. It's completely decentralized so there's no need for any central authority to set regulations to the exchange rate.

It's a great currency that will continue to revolutionize the way we trade in the world. It's still a new concept that is slowly being understood and accepted by a large number of businesses and merchants all across the economies in the world.

There's an increase in the amount of investments that will bring new financial companies that will offer their expertise and consumer friendly solutions in order for the currency to be used every day.

There are some advantages and disadvantages that Bitcoin has. Even though the verification process takes a bit of time to process and the volatility levels are relatively high at the moment, with time the levels of rapid fluctuations will stabilize as the market grows in size. The risks that are included with the currency will later on be mitigated as more investors and consumers learn and understand the use of bitcoins.

The bitcoin market has made so much progress from the time of its creation and development back in the year of 2009 by the original creator who is still a mystery. But nevertheless, the bitcoin market will remain in use for a long time, or until the cap limit is reached. Its evolution is still in progress and has much more room for improvements and growth within the next few years. Within the next few years, many companies will have adopted the currency to their acceptable payment methods. The Bitcoin wallet will also have better security measures to ensure the Bitcoin owner privacy and security. All in all, the Bitcoin currency will continue to integrate itself into the global financial system.

Now that you've understood how to the Bitcoin market works, you can be able to get your feet wet and try earning some bitcoins for yourself.

Trade well and be successful.

www.ingramcontent.com/pod-product-compliance
Lightning Source LLC
Chambersburg PA
CBHW071816170526
45167CB00003B/1322